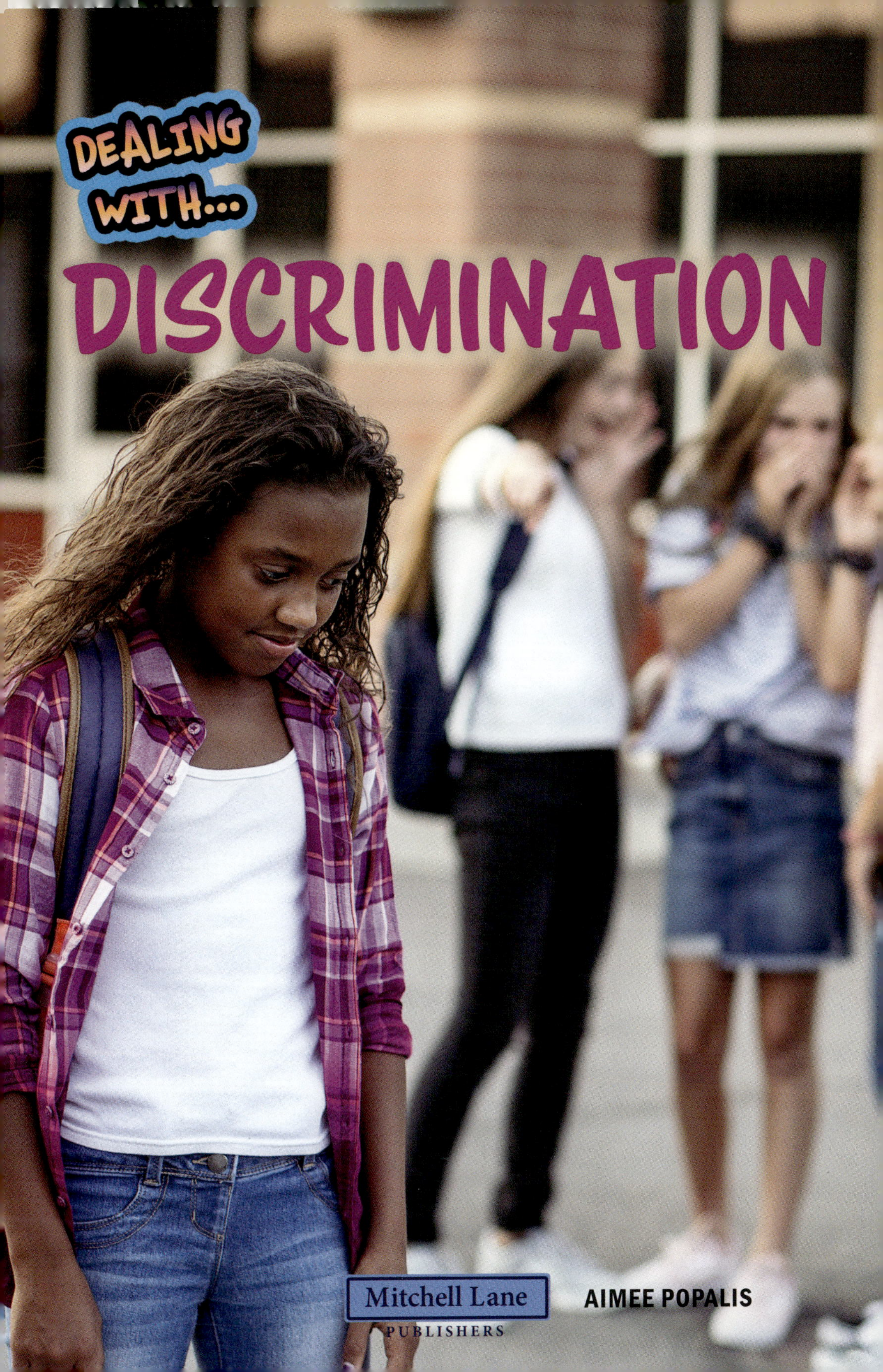

DEALING WITH...

# DISCRIMINATION

AIMEE POPALIS

Mitchell Lane
PUBLISHERS

## Parent and Caregiver Tips for Creating Nonfiction Readers

Timely topics in the *Dealing With...* series will interest intermediate and middle school readers and equip them with helpful strategies for coping with difficult situations. Your reader will be introduced to new concepts, facts, ideas, and vocabulary.

## Tips for Reading Nonfiction

### Talk about Nonfiction

Explain that nonfiction books provide facts about real-world topics. When readers read nonfiction, they gain a rich understanding of the world. They build background knowledge that provides a foundation for learning and academic success.

### Look at the Parts

This book contains the following helpful features. Share the purpose of each feature with your reader.

***Photos, Captions, and Graphic Aids***
The photos, captions, charts, and other graphic aids in nonfiction texts contain a wealth of information. Help your reader identify different ways information can be displayed.

***Sidebars***
These extra tidbits of information help satisfy readers' curiosity and expand their knowledge.

***Table of Contents***
Located at the front of the book, this list shows the big ideas within the text and the page numbers where they can be found.

***Extension Activities and Additional Resources***
A "Your Turn" quiz and "Exploration and Discovery" activities invite readers to apply their new knowledge. Supporting resources are provided in a special "You Are Not Alone" section.

***Glossary***
Located at the back of the book, the glossary defines key words and phrases that are related to the topic. These words and phrases can be found in the text in **bold** type.

***Index***
Located at the back of the book, the index is an alphabetical list of topics and the page numbers where they can be found.

With a little help and guidance, your reader will be on their way to enjoying and learning from nonfiction books.

Mitchell Lane
PUBLISHERS
mitchelllanepub.com

2001 SW 31st Avenue
Hallandale, FL 33009



First Edition, 2026.
Author: Aimee Popalis
Designer: Rhea Magaro
Editor: Kim Thompson

Series: Dealing With...
Title: Dealing with Discrimination / by Aimee Popalis

Hallandale, FL : Mitchell Lane Publishers, [2026]

Library bound ISBN: 979-8-89260-672-1
eBook ISBN: 979-8-89260-681-3

PHOTO CREDITS
Dreamstime: Galina Barskaya, 5, 41; Shutterstock: Brocreative, cover, 1; Oksana Klymenko, 6; Pixel-Shot, 7; Szasz-Fabian Jozsef, 8; Motortion Films, 9; Simple Line, 10; DOERS, 11; IdeaGeneration, 12; earth phakphum, 13; archivector, 14; MAYA LAB, 14; Vitalii Vodolazskyi, 15; Gorodenkoff, 16; New Africa, 17; Julia Manga, 18; Michail Petrov, 19; fizkes, 20; Jovica Varga, 21; Ground Picture, 22; Annavish, 23; VGstockstudio, 24; Mastaco, 25; Ainul muttaqin, 26; 1000 Words 27; Antonov Maxim, 29; pakww, 30; kowition, 30; BearFotos, 31; Studio Romantic, 32; SylisiaDesign, 33; Faizal Ramli, 34; Sam72, 35; Africa Studio, 36; Studio113, 37; AYO Production, 38; iofoto, 42; OSTILL is Franck Camhi, 44; Sergey Novikov, 47

# Table of Contents

**Chapter 1:** Food for Thought ........................................4

**Chapter 2:** What Is Discrimination? ........................8

Types of Discrimination

Discrimination and the Brain

Discrimination and Individual Differences

**Chapter 3:** Signs of Discrimination........................18

Is This Discrimination?

Effects of Discrimination

When Is Discrimination a Problem?

**Chapter 4:** Strategies for Taking Control.................. 28

Strategy #1: Be Mindful

Strategy #2: Stand Up for Yourself

Strategy #3: Find Your Friends

Strategy #4: Take Action

Strategy #5: Be Kind to Yourself

Strategy #6: Walk Away...Or Choose to Stay

**Chapter 5:** Dealing with Discrimination .................. 40

Your Turn: How Do You Deal with Discrimination? .......... 42

Exploration and Discovery: Activities to Try ................ 43

You Are Not Alone.............................................. 44

Glossary ................................................................ 46

Index...................................................................... 48

About the Author .................................................... 48

# Chapter 1: Food for Thought

## Fatima

Fatima heard noises coming from the next table in the cafeteria. She looked up from her lunch to see kids staring at her.

One girl held her nose dramatically. A boy pretended to gag. Fatima could hear some of what the kids were saying.

"Ew! That's just gross!"

"How can she eat that?"

"Dare you to ask her for a bite."

Fatima turned back to her lunch. Her face burned with embarrassment. The food that had looked delicious when she packed it this morning now seemed different.

That day, Fatima had brought something special for lunch. It was a dish her grandmother had taught her mom how to make. It was filled with spices and memories of her family. Usually, Fatima loved it. Now, she began to close the container and hide the food away.

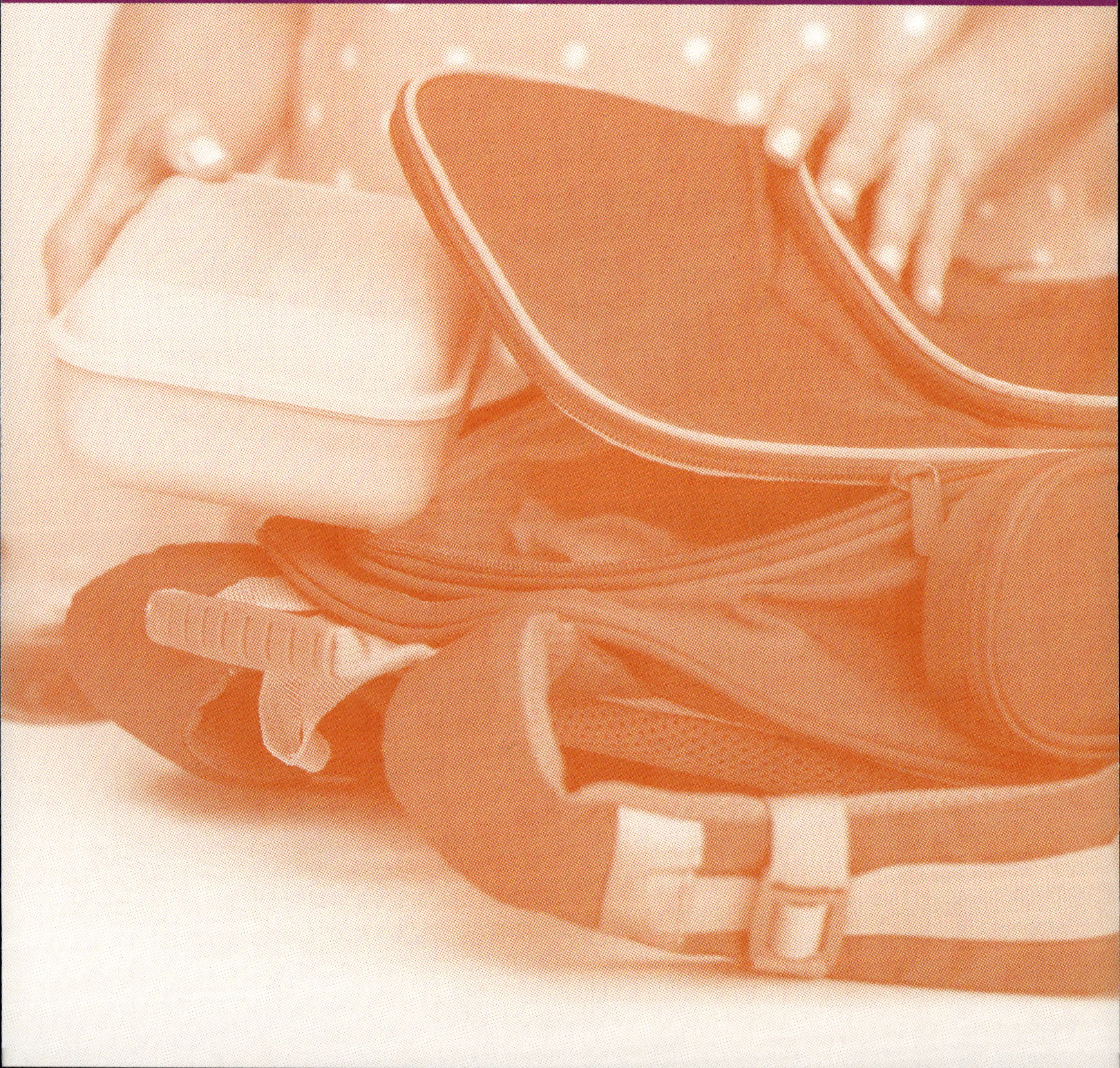

Just then, her friend Maya arrived. "Done already?" Maya asked.

Fatima wasn't sure what to say. *Would Maya make fun of her too?* she worried.

## What Do You Think?

- Why does Fatima think about her food differently after hearing her classmates' comments?
- Why does Fatima want to hide her food? What other choices does she have?
- Should other people's opinions change how you feel about yourself?
- Have you ever been treated like Fatima was or seen someone treated this way? What did you do?

# Chapter 2: What Is Discrimination?

**Discrimination** is treating a person or a group of people unfairly because of who they are. It happens when people believe that others are not as good as them or don't deserve respect. Discrimination is wrong. Everyone deserves to be treated with **dignity**, even if they are different than you.

It feels awful to be treated unfairly, especially if it is because of something that you can't change or wouldn't want to change. These reasons can include what you look like, what you believe, or where you come from. If someone treats you differently because of who you are, it's not your fault. You have a right to feel proud and confident.

# Types of Discrimination

Discrimination happens in different ways and for different reasons. It can happen in real life or online. All discrimination hurts people by making them feel less valued, excluded, or even unsafe. When discrimination repeatedly scares, hurts, or bothers someone on purpose, it is **bullying**.

People can be discriminated against for anything that makes them seem different. Some common reasons for discrimination include:

- ☐ Skin color, race, or **ethnicity**
- ☐ Gender
- ☐ Age
- ☐ Ability
- ☐ Religion
- ☐ Culture
- ☐ Appearance
- ☐ How much money someone's family has

RAISE YOUR VOICE

### There IS Good News!

A *bystander* watches discrimination and does nothing to stop or discourage it. Bystanders are part of the problem. You can choose to be an *upstander* who takes action to help. You can say something like, "That's not funny!" Most of the time, this quickly stops the unfair treatment.

# Discrimination and the Brain

Your brain is always working to keep you safe and happy. It makes choices based on things you've learned from family and friends, from your own experiences, and from your fears and concerns. Based on this information, your brain creates shortcuts. It comes up with **generalizations** it uses to decide what's good or bad, safe or not.

Sometimes, these shortcuts are helpful. For example, you know that if you are explaining something to a little kid, you need to use simpler words. But sometimes, your brain's shortcuts can lead to mistakes in judgment. Relying on shortcuts can cause you to have unfair thoughts about things or people you don't know well.

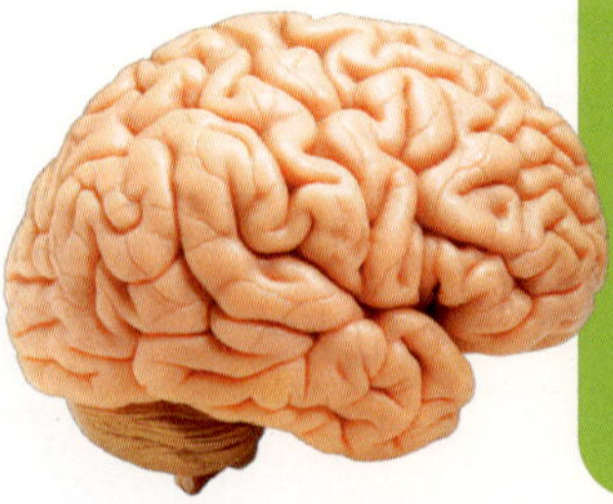

## Studies Show That...

You make over 30,000 decisions every day! To make those decisions quickly, your brain relies on patterns and shortcuts.

Your brain creates shortcuts without you even noticing. A generalization you aren't aware of is called a **bias**. People's biases can make them think and act as if something is true, even if there is no proof. For example, you might believe your favorite sports team is the best. This bias could cause you to ignore the talents of other teams, even if they are just as good. A bias can make you see things differently than they really are, without considering all the facts.

**Prejudice** is a strong, negative bias about a group of people who are different than you. Being prejudiced means judging others without knowing them. For example, someone might think all people from a certain country are bad, even if they've never met anyone from there.

### Studies Show That...

When you don't know someone, your brain makes guesses about them to fill in the blanks. The guesses can be wrong. They can make you fear people or feel uneasy around them.

## Did You Know?

A **stereotype** is a generalization about how you expect people to look or act. Many characters in movies and TV shows are based on stereotypes. Thinking that all tall people play basketball is an example of a stereotype. Very often, stereotypes are wrong. They can hurt people's feelings. Instead of assuming that people fit stereotypes, it's better to get to know them as they really are.

People often learn biases and prejudices from their families, their communities, and the media. These false beliefs are hard to change because feeling like you are better than others can boost **self-esteem**. Everyone wants to believe they look and act *the right way*. Thinking that others are wrong can help people feel confident that they are right.

# Discrimination and Individual Differences

In any group, having **diversity** is an advantage. A diverse group includes a variety of people who are different than each other.

When people accept and appreciate each other's differences, amazing things happen! They learn new things, make new friends, and become kinder and more understanding. You wouldn't want to live in a world where everyone is the same. You would miss out on the benefit of other people's unique talents, ideas, and perspectives.

## There Is Good News!

Movies, books, TV shows, and ads are getting better at including people with a variety of skin colors, abilities, languages, and cultures. Everyone should feel like they belong!

# Chapter 3: Signs of Discrimination

Recognizing the signs of discrimination can help you stand up for yourself and others. It can also help you be fairer and more **inclusive** in your own actions.

**Discrimination can sound like:**

- ☐ Hurtful comments or jokes
- ☐ The spreading of stereotypes or false information about a person or group of people
- ☐ Slurs or name-calling
- ☐ Mean or personal questions

**Discrimination can look like:**

- ☐ Excluding someone from conversations or activities
- ☐ Unkind social media posts
- ☐ Pushing, hitting, or physical intimidation
- ☐ Making rude gestures or mocking someone's speech or movements
- ☐ Setting unfair rules or expectations

**Discrimination can feel like:**

- ☐ Worry or fear
- ☐ Sadness
- ☐ Confusion
- ☐ Embarrassment
- ☐ Loneliness
- ☐ A headache, stomachache, or other physical discomfort

Discrimination can happen to anyone at any time. It can be hard to spot. How do you know if you are being discriminated against? Trust your feelings. They can help you identify unfair treatment, even when it's not obvious.

## Did You Know?

Microaggressions are small words or actions that have a big impact. *Micro* means "tiny," and *aggression* means "attack." Examples of microaggressions are joking about the way someone talks or ignoring someone's ideas. Even though they seem small, microaggressions can make people feel uncomfortable or unwelcome.

Discriminatory actions or words may be disguised as jokes or simple comments. If something doesn't seem right about the way you are being treated, or if you feel uncomfortable, pay attention. What other people say and do shouldn't make you feel scared, sad, or confused.

# Is This Discrimination?

Not everything that feels unfair is discrimination. Sometimes, things just don't go your way. Here are some questions to help you tell the difference.

- ☐ Am I being treated differently for no clear reason?
- ☐ Is this happening because of who I am (like my race, religion, or gender)?
- ☐ Does this keep happening, even when I follow the rules?
- ☐ Are my abilities or efforts being ignored because of who I am?
- ☐ Does this make me feel bad about myself?

Remember, discrimination is when someone treats you unfairly because of *who you are*. Sometimes, people's decisions about you relate to things you can change and improve, like your choices, skills, and behavior. This can be frustrating, but it is not discrimination. Talking to a trusted adult can help you better understand your situation.

# Effects of Discrimination

When people treat you like you don't matter, you might start to believe it. Discrimination can change the way people see themselves. It can lower their confidence or make them feel like they don't belong. Discrimination can make it harder for people to try new things, make friends, or do well in school.

Facing discrimination doesn't just hurt your feelings. It affects your brain and body too. Dealing with discrimination causes **stress**. Over time, stress impacts your health. It makes you feel tired and unfocused. It causes stomachaches, headaches, and sore muscles. It can lead to serious mental health challenges like **anxiety** and **depression**.

# When Is Discrimination a Problem?

Discrimination is always a problem. It is never okay. It is especially harmful when it affects someone's safety, the way they feel about themselves, or the opportunities available to them. All people deserve **equality** and safety and the right to be themselves.

Remember, if people are being unfair or unkind because of who you are, it is not your fault. You are not alone. There are many people and organizations that work to end discrimination in schools, businesses, and communities. **Activists** are people who try to change rules and laws so they are fair to everyone. You can be an activist too. Speak up if you see discrimination. Help to educate others. All actions make a difference!

### Did You Know?

A serious, dangerous, or violent form of discrimination is called a hate crime. Special laws make sure these severe actions have big consequences.

NO PLACE FOR HATE
NO TO RACISM
NO TO RACISM
IST

# Chapter 4: Strategies for Taking Control

Experiencing discrimination is challenging for anyone. While you can't control other people's behavior, you can control how you react. Try these strategies to help you find the best way to deal with discrimination.

## Strategy #1: Be Mindful

Practicing **mindfulness** has many benefits. It works like a pause button, giving you time to think clearly and make better decisions. By focusing on what you are sensing in the moment, you feel more confident and in control of tough situations. Try these techniques.

### Did You Know?

Olympic athletes, NASA astronauts, and NFL players use mindfulness techniques to manage stress and help them perform their best.

## Box Breathing

Sit or stand in a relaxed but alert position. Then, cycle through these four steps. Repeat until you feel calmer and more relaxed.

1. Breathe in slowly and deeply while counting to four.
2. Gently hold your breath for a count of four.
3. Breathe out while counting to four.
4. Pause for a count of four.

## Sensory Focus

When you are upset, focusing on your five senses can help you feel better. Connecting with your senses reminds your brain that you're okay. Follow these steps.

1. Look at something closely. It could be a piece of art, the sky, or a tree. Notice details.
2. Touch something nearby. Is it hard or soft? Warm or cool?
3. Listen carefully. Notice the quietest sound.
4. Take a sip of water and pay attention as it moves from your lips to your throat.
5. Breathe in deeply and notice what you can smell.

# Strategy #2: Stand up for Yourself

Speaking up to someone who is unkind can be scary, but it's a powerful way to protect yourself and support others. Try these techniques.

## Return to Sender

Refuse to accept discrimination! Respond to someone's discriminatory words or actions with a question. This shifts the focus back to them and makes them reflect on the consequences of their actions. Ask questions like these.

- ☐ Can you repeat that, please?
- ☐ What makes you say that?
- ☐ What did you mean by that?

## Assertive Statements

Being assertive means saying what you think clearly and honestly. It shows that you are confident and that you value yourself. It teaches others to treat you with respect.

If you feel safe, calmly tell others when their words or actions are wrong. Using simple, assertive statements can stop discrimination without making things worse. Try these statements.

- ☐ Please don't talk that way to me or anyone else.
- ☐ What you are saying is wrong. You need to stop.
- ☐ When you do that, I feel...
- ☐ That was a hurtful thing to say. I think you are nicer than that.

# Strategy #3: Find Your Friends

Spending time with supportive people makes a big difference. Connecting with friends boosts your happiness and reduces stress. It even improves your health by calming your heart rate and increasing your energy level.

Talking with friends can help you find solutions to tough problems. Feeling like you belong to a group can help you face challenges with confidence.

Your supporters can include teachers, coaches, family members, and other adults. Their guidance can help you get through tough times.

# Strategy #4: Take Action

Discrimination can make you feel powerless. Empower yourself by speaking up and working to solve the problem. Find ways to remind yourself and others that everyone deserves to be treated fairly and with respect. Try these techniques.

## Know Your Rights

Schools and communities have policies to make sure everyone is treated equally. Take time to learn about your rights. Find out what rules, laws, and procedures protect you. Teachers and family members can help you do research and understand what you read. Being confident about your rights makes it easier to speak up, ask for help, or take a stand.

## Find Your Voice

It takes courage to speak up, but it is one of the best ways to stop discrimination. Your voice matters, and it can make a difference. Keep spreading your message until you are heard. You will help make your school or community better for everyone! Try these strategies.

- ☐ Tell a trusted adult.
- ☐ Write to someone in charge, like a principal, business owner, or government official.
- ☐ Start or join an organization that promotes equality.
- ☐ Write an article or blog post that educates others about discrimination.
- ☐ Make posters or artwork to raise awareness.
- ☐ Keep a record of repeated discrimination.

# Strategy #5: Be Kind to Yourself

You don't need to wait for others to make you feel better. You can be kind and supportive to yourself! Treat yourself well, even when others don't. Try these techniques.

## Positive Self-Talk

What you tell yourself is more important than what others say to you. Using positive self-talk means thinking kind, encouraging thoughts about yourself. Find a phrase that makes you feel confident. Repeat it often. Words such as *I am loved* and *I am proud of who I am* are powerful tools to help you feel your best.

## Favorite Things

Take time to do what you love. Draw, write, play music, exercise, practice a sport, or hang out with friends. These activities will help you relax, express yourself, process information, and manage your emotions. They will remind you of your strengths and boost your self-esteem. As a bonus, connecting with others who share your interests will help you make new friends and build a support network.

# Strategy #6: Walk Away... Or Choose to Stay

If you find yourself in an unfair or unwelcoming situation, sometimes the best thing you can do is walk away. Go and look for friends and places that make you feel happy and appreciated. You are amazing! The best people accept you for who you are.

It's also okay to stay, especially if you love what you're doing! Don't let others tell you what you can or can't do. If someone is being unfair, stay calm. Be kind to yourself. Talk to a trusted adult who can help.

Whatever you choose, stay true to yourself. Take pride in your decision.

Sometimes, you don't get to choose who you're around. You have to go to school and deal with your family members. In those moments, focus on the good people in your life. If you feel unsafe, talk to someone you trust right away!

# Chapter 5: Dealing with Discrimination

Remember Fatima? As she packed up her lunch, her friend Maya sat down. "That looks good," Maya said. "If you're not going to eat it, can I try it?"

Fatima was surprised, but hopeful. She offered Maya a taste. Her friend's eyes lit up. "Wow," Maya said. "That's amazing!"

Fatima smiled and felt braver. Maybe she didn't need to hide her food. Maybe she just needed to share it with the right people. Fatima made a mental note to invite Maya to come to her house for dinner sometime.

The next time kids at school made fun of her lunch, Fatima took a deep breath. She said calmly, "It's okay if it doesn't look good to you. I think it's delicious. And millions of people agree with me. You can try a bite if you want."

The other kids fell silent. Fatima felt a rush of confidence. She knew she had nothing to be ashamed of.

**Remember:** Discrimination is based on false ideas and bad guesses. It is not your fault. You have a right to be you!

# YOUR TURN: HOW DO YOU DEAL WITH DISCRIMINATION?

For each situation, select the answer most likely to produce the best outcome. Make a note of your answers on a separate sheet of paper.

1. Marie and her friend Reese want to join the school's robotics team. The fees are expensive, and Reese's family can't afford it. What should Marie do?
   - **A.** Tell Reese you hope her parents change their minds. It's not that much.
   - **B.** Help Reese raise money by doing yardwork together for neighbors.
   - **C.** Talk to your school administrator about creating scholarship opportunities. Everyone deserves a chance to do what they love.

2. Armondo uses a wheelchair. His classmates often leave him out of games outside or in the gym because they assume he can't keep up or participate. Armondo really wants to play. How can he change his classmates' minds?
   - **A.** Remind himself that he deserves to play and talk to a teacher who can help students better understand his abilities.
   - **B.** Avoid the situation and watch games from the sidelines.
   - **C.** Yell at his classmates and tell them they're being mean.

3. Gabby's friend posts a video mocking people who speak English with an accent. Gabby is upset because most of her family members speak with an accent. How should Gabby address this with her friend?
   - **A.** Ignore it but avoid letting her friend spend time with her family.
   - **B.** Explain to her friend why the post was hurtful and ask her to delete it.
   - **C.** Make fun of her friend's family.

4. Jordan notices that the school library has very few books with characters from different cultures. How can Jordan help the school offer a more diverse selection of books?
   - **A.** Talk to a friend to see if they've noticed the same thing.
   - **B.** Check out books with more diversity from the public library.
   - **C.** Write to the librarian and principal, explaining the importance of offering diverse books and suggesting specific titles to add to the collection.

**Think about your answers.**

1. The best answer is C. Encouraging the school to create scholarships helps everyone, not just Reese, have a chance to join the team.
2. The best answer is A. Using positive self-talk and getting help from a teacher can give Armondo the support he needs to change his classmates' biases.
3. The best answer is B. Being assertive and telling her friend how she feels helps Gabby stand up for her family and explain why the video is hurtful.
4. The best answer is C. Writing to the people in charge is the best way to make them aware of the lack of diversity in the library and inspire them to make it better.

## EXPLORATION AND DISCOVERY: ACTIVITIES TO TRY

1. Create a self-portrait. Fill the margins with words that describe all the things that make you unique. Hang it where you will see it often.
2. Find a role model. It could be someone famous or someone you know. Write three things that you admire about your role model and that will inspire you in tough times.
3. Find a quote about equality or diversity that inspires you. Make a short video sharing the quote and what it means to you. Talk to your parents about options for posting it online.
4. Interview family members or friends. Find out if they have ever experienced discrimination. What happened? How did they resolve it?
5. Write a letter to yourself to read during difficult times. Remind yourself of some of the best things about you and the good things you have in your life.

# YOU ARE NOT ALONE

Experiencing discrimination can make you feel hopeless and alone. But you are NOT alone. There are good people who care about you and want to help. There are also many resources you can use to learn more and help yourself.

Explore some of these ways to find the kindness and support you deserve.

**People to Ask for Help**

☑ guidance counselor
☑ teacher
☑ principal
☑ assistant principal
☑ parent
☑ older sibling
☑ grandparent
☑ aunt or uncle
☑ coach
☑ school secretary
☑ bus driver
☑ religious youth group leader
☑ any friend that you trust
☑ any adult that you trust

## Websites

Childline: Discrimination, Hate Crime and Equality
www.childline.org.uk/info-advice/bullying-abuse-safety/your-rights/discrimination-hate-crime-equality
Learn about discrimination and equality and find advice on standing up for your rights.

DoSomething.org
dosomething.org
Explore opportunities to take action on a variety of social issues.

Kids Helpline: Dealing with Discrimination
kidshelpline.com.au/teens/issues/dealing-discrimination
Explore strategies for dealing with discrimination of all kinds.

---

## Books


Gonzalez, Maribel Valdez. *Be Your True Self (Social Justice and You)*. Capstone Press, 2022.

McGhee, Heather. *The Sum of Us: How Racism Hurts Everyone (Adapted for Young Readers)*. Yearling, 2024.

Tottingham, Ryse (ed.). *The Young Activist's Dictionary of Social Justice*. Duopress, 2022.


---

## Phone Helplines

Crisis Text Line
Text HOME to 741741 or message on WhatsApp. Young people of color can text STEVE to 741741 to reach culturally trained counselors.

LGBT National Youth Talkline
1-800-246-7743

National Suicide Prevention Lifeline
1-800-273-8255

Suicide and Crisis Lifeline
Call or text 988.

# GLOSSARY

**activists** (AK-tuh-vists)
People who support a cause and take action to change things

**anxiety** (ang-ZYE-i-tee)
Feelings of worry or fear

**bias** (BYE-uhs)
A tendency to notice or favor one thing over another

**bullying** (BUL-ee-ing)
Being mean to someone on purpose

**depression** (di-PRESH-uhn)
Unhappiness that doesn't go away

**dignity** (DIG-ni-tee)
Having the respect or esteem of others

**discrimination** (dis-krim-i-NAY-shuhn)
Unfair treatment of someone because they are different

**diversity** (di-VUR-si-tee)
Having a variety; not being all the same

**equality** (i-KWAH-li-tee)
The right of all people to be treated the same

**ethnicity** (eth-NI-suh-tee)
People with a common history, culture, or race; the racial or ethnic group you belong to

**generalizations** (JEN-ur-uh-li-zay-shuhns)

Broad statements that get applied to everyone or everything, often incorrectly

**inclusive** (in-KLOO-siv)

Welcoming to everyone

**mindfulness** (MINDE-fuhl-nis)

The practice of focusing your attention on the present moment

**prejudice** (PREJ-uh-dis)

An opinion or idea formed unfairly or without having all the facts

**self-esteem** (self i-STEEM)

How someone thinks about themself and their capabilities

**stereotype** (STER-ee-oh-tipe)

A widely held idea, opinion, or image of a person, group, or thing; stereotypes are overly simple and often untrue

**stress** (stres)

Worry, strain, or pressure

# INDEX


bias 13–15

bullying 10

bystander 11

diversity 16

family 6, 10, 12, 33, 34, 38

feelings 15, 20, 25, 33

friends 12, 16, 24, 33, 37, 38

microaggressions 21

prejudice 14, 15

race 10, 22

school 24, 26, 34, 35, 38, 40

stress 25, 28, 33


# ABOUT THE AUTHOR

**Aimee Popalis** is a teacher, mom, and book lover living in Tampa, Florida. She loves to read stories about different people and cultures. Her appreciation of these stories, along with the diverse backgrounds of her students, inspires her to write about important topics like fairness and inclusivity. Aimee believes that everyone's stories and perspectives are valuable and make the world a beautiful and interesting place. When she's not writing or teaching, you can find her exploring nature with her family or lost in a good book.